Oh SLAP!

MY CHOICES DETERMINE MY DESTINY!

A Guide to Making Better Choices
and Living a Self-Empowered Life

LORI GENTLES

Oh Slap! My Choices Determine My Destiny!

Scriptures references in this book are from the King James Version (KJV), public domain.

Cover illustration by Tara Thelen
Design by Deborah Perdue, Illumination Grapics
Stock art courtesy of shutterstock.com and depositphotos.com

Paperback ISBN: 978-0-578-80952-6

DEDICATION

· ·

To my mother, who is one of the smartest people I know and who taught me the value of common sense in navigating this nonsensical world.

To my father, who made the choice to be happy every day until the day he died. May he rest in peace.

CONTENTS

Introduction 1

Confession 3

Disclaimer 6

Warning 7

Target 8

Last Chance 10

Summary 12

Part 1: Your Personal Life—It All Starts with You . 15

Chapter 1—It's Up to You, Boo! 17

Chapter 2—Whatcha Gonna Do Now?. 29

Chapter 3—Mind Your Damn Business 37

Chapter 4—Get Off Your Big Fat But[t]. 43

Chapter 5—Embrace Your Power 49

Part 2: Your Work Life—Understand the Contract . 55

Chapter 6—Conspiracy Theory 57

Chapter 7—Yo Momma Don't Work Here 63

Chapter 8—Encore. 81

Chapter 9—It's Not Your Boss's Fault, Fool 85

Chapter 10—Obstruction Junction 89

Part 3: Your Future Life—Don't Ask, Just Do! . . 93

Chapter 11—Positive Rebellion? Hell, Yes! 95

**Bonus Tips, Quips, and Other Radical
and Random Rants** 101

ACKNOWLEDGMENT

Thanks to all the good and positive people in my life. You affirm that the universe is on my side. I would be remiss if I didn't also give thanks for negative forces that have passed through my life. Your presence brought discomfort and motivated me to action. I am grateful because "All things are working together for my good."

INTRODUCTION

'm so excited for you. If you are brave enough to read this book and apply even a few of the lessons learned, your life will change for the better. I can say this with certainty because you cannot unring a bell. Even if you don't immediately apply what you learn (which would be a shame, to delay your own progress and happiness), seeds will be planted within you that will someday be cultivated and flourish, if you allow them to.

Do not read this book if your heart is not eagerly beating for change; if your being—your soul—is not yearning to blossom; if your soil isn't fertile, if you're unwilling to grow, if you're a notorious resister of change; or worse yet, if you think you have actualized. Those who believe they have self-actualized are worse off because they believe they know it all. They are unconsciously incompetent—a fancy term that means *stupid*.

***Stupidity** is not the lack of knowledge, but the illusion of having it.*

—Grigore Julian

This inane thought makes you juvenile—like the arrogant pimple-faced kid with an attitude who mocks you for trying to drop a bit of wisdom because, of course, he knows it all. Here's a little wisdom for you. You never arrive (unless perhaps in death, but who can say)—you simply continue to evolve. It's a journey. So buckle up and stop asking, "Are we there yet?"

CONFESSION

That being said, I must confess that this book was born of frustration. And some parts of the book might sound downright angry. More about my anger issues later. My frustration stems from the multiple decades I've spent working with people who I *know* possess personal genius but are not "woke" to it. They shy away from their brilliance due to low self-esteem, a result of negative and limiting belief structures developed in childhood, reinforced and perpetuated by their own repeated self-declarations of lack, societal expectations, laziness, and herd mentality. They have given in and given up.

In some respects, the workplace is a laboratory that fosters this behavior. It is like a schoolyard. The kid who stands out by going above and beyond is mocked, criticized, and ostracized; labeled a goody two shoes. Just as in the schoolyard, it is not encouraged to stand out too much in the workplace—or so the limiting belief (aka *lie*) goes. I know fully mature adults (agewise, that is) who are highly immature when it comes to their level of being. They behave inauthentically, ignoring or never recognizing their purpose on this earth and robbing the rest of us of their brilliance. Many truly are the walking dead—unplugged and unwired.

Have you ever worked in a place where you could've sworn you were in an alternate universe? The way people behave, their thought processes, the decisions they make are so illogical and nonsensical, even in the face of compelling facts. You begin to think, *Where the hell am I? Am I actually in hell? Maybe it does exist!* I've been in this situation more often than I'd like, and

I believe the reason is because we primarily operate with our robotic brain.

We've been programmed from the beginning with all sorts of messages from our families, coworkers, the media, preachers, teachers, and friends, who all reinforce "going with the grain"—go along to get along, don't stand out too much, don't be too good, and don't even *think* about being great. What are you trying to do, make the rest of us look bad? This type of programming denies authenticity and rewards herdism.

I know this programming well, on a deeply personal level. I'll spare you the gritty and salacious details of my childhood story. In short, I was the seventh of eight children, father suffered from drinking too much, mother made ends meet with public assistance, both high school educated. I, being the first generation college grad, was simultaneously celebrated, ridiculed, ostracized, and told that I thought I was better than everyone else in my family—presumably because I "got a little knowledge."

Growing up, I was told that I was stupid and that I would never have any friends. I don't remember being told "I love you" as a child, it just wasn't said freely in my family. Maybe it was said, but the phrase "You are stupid" has a way of drowning out anything that follows. There was a five-year gap between my brother, the sixth child, and me. Every child before that was just a year a part. Then finally, a break—five years pregnancy free. My siblings were growing up and my parents had more freedom.

Then dagnammit, my mom is pregnant again—with moi. One more mouth to feed. Call me psychic, but I'm pretty sure I was not planned. Hearing "I wish you were never born" and "I hate you" was my clue. My grandmother, on the other hand, said that I was special. She was a chubby, superstitious lady who smelled of bleach from cleaning people's homes for a living. She believed in numerology, astrology and other related ologies.

The number seven is auspicious. It's a holy number to some, the angel number to others. It symbolizes all positive and valuable conditions, like prosperity, life, happiness, renewal, and perfection. Some numerologists believe that the number seven is so perfect and powerful that it represents a connection to the universe.

And because I was the seventh child—well, do I need to say more? Truth be told, it was my grandma who was the special one. My grandmother was everything I needed to spur me on to success. She died the summer before my freshman year of college. Amid the negative, reductive, and limiting messages I heard as a child, I chose to believe my grandmother. Did you catch that? I *chose*. That's not to say the limiting beliefs didn't interfere with my levels of success—I should be a multimillionaire by now.

But I only recently discovered that some of my beliefs were limiting. You see, because I was told that I thought I was better than everyone else, I tried not to be better. I tried to dumb down, not be too good, and dim my enthusiasm for enlightenment. I tried to moderate my success, to shrink and become small. I bought into the lie that I'm a regular person with regular beliefs. I failed to realize that I am an extraordinary person with the ability to create an extraordinary life.

In his book, *The Hero Effect: Being Your Best When It Matters the Most*, Kevin Brown says, "We were all born extraordinary and we made choices to become ordinary along the way." You don't have to be the seventh child in your family to know that you were created in the image of perfection. Unfortunately, we choose to be ordinary, suppressing our greatness just to fit in.

What's your story? Where in your life have you found yourself shrinking, hiding your genius, becoming small?

_____

_____

_____

_____

_____

DISCLAIMER

I am not a sadist or a masochist. I always forget which one is which—but I'm neither, for the record. However, I do believe that without some discomfort, without some level of pain, there is no growth. One of my fitness coaches always barked, "Results are not made in the comfort zone." Get ready to be uncomfortable.

This is not a friendly, coddling, sugary book that tells you you're perfect just as you are. Although, if you *are* happy with where you're at in your life and your career, then fantastic—you *should* feel good—fist in the air, pump three times. But I suspect that if you purchased this book (or someone gave it to you), you are interested in elevating your life experiences—or someone thinks you should be (hint, hint).

WARNING

Did you read the title? You might find that you are jolted into soberness like a swift slap on the face with the straightforward, no-bullshit talk that might cause you a twinge of pain. You might find yourself saying "ouch" or "amen" as you read certain sections. That's a good sign. It means that the information is resonating with you on some level. It's stirring something within you. If you allow yourself to sit with the pain, to examine why it's manifesting as it is, you will get closer to your truth.

Notice I said *your truth*, because it is not my truth. Everyone has his or her own road to travel and the truth is what is true for you. Then it is up to you to act on your increased level of consciousness. If you run away from the twinge, the temporary moment of discomfort, congratulations, you have just reupped for average and secured your spot in the mediocre club.

*Intelligent **individuals learn** from every thing and every one;*
***average people**, from their **experiences**.*
The stupid already have all the answers.
—Socrates

Don't hate the high achievers for doing what you wouldn't do but had every opportunity to do. Those folks will far exceed you on almost every dimension. It's only the exceptional who will have the courage and stamina to be audacious, do what most won't—that is to examine the hard stuff. Gay Hendricks, author of *The Big Leap: Conquer Your Hidden Fear and Take Your Life to the Next Level*, says that "Going into your inner depths, where your most deeply held beliefs about what's possible reside, counts in my book as a radical act."

Are you ready to get radical? Well, come on, let's get naked then. Don't get too excited. I'm not talking about showing off your birthday suit. Although showing off what your mama gave you might be easier than what this book will challenge you to do. You will need to become a stripper. Stripping psychologically and spiritually down to your prebirth status—your spiritual self. What your spirit knows you are.

Your spirit is boundless, confident, all capable, fearless, existing before you had a physical body, and godlike. We are, after all, made in God's image. Your ego is prideful, restricting, limiting, fearful, full of shame and guilt, desirous of approval so much so that you are willing to be fake to get approval. The boundaries that bind you will be exposed as you read this book. You will need to suspend all that you think you know.

TARGET

As stated previously, this book was borne of my frustration with people I came across in the workplace. Many of them were completely out of touch with their purpose in life. This misalignment created depression, poor conduct, bitterness, unhappiness, passive aggressiveness, jealousy, and minimalism—not the good environmental kind but the doing-the-bare-minimum-to-get-a-paycheck-and-not-get-fired kind. The idea that "I must endure fifteen more years of misery until I retire and collect my inadequate pension" is a disempowering thought.

I hyperventilate when I hear people say they hate their jobs but they have fifteen more years to retirement. I can't breathe. It's unfathomable that people trade their joy in life for money. Their miserable state is manifested in chronic griping, complaining, gossiping about everything, but mostly their boss or the management. They have no idea that they, and they alone, might be creating and reinforcing this negative and toxic reality and that they have a choice.

Jen Sincero, author of *You Are a Badass at Making Money: Master the Mindset of Wealth*, said, "Time wasted rationalizing the mediocre could be time spent creating the magnificent." Ironically, these people believe they have no choice, yet choose with every act to continue believing that their state of misery is everyone else's fault. To be honest, I can hardly tolerate this victim behavior displayed by some individuals. So I have chosen to do something about it—try to change the status quo by inspiring people to act, to take risks and create a different future for themselves by practicing iChoice—intelligent, inspired, intentional, individual choice.

I've discovered that one of my purposes is to help uplift and uplevel highly motivated individuals to greater levels of achievement. So this book is targeted toward the highly motivated individual at any stage and level in their personal, professional, or educational career. Even the highest-level leaders will grow from this book. Some of the highest-ranking individuals are most in need of this message. Successful people are often victims of their success. The more successful you already are, the more you might be enslaved to your ego instead of being free with your spirit. Your spirit cannot hurt you. No matter where you are in life, as long as you open up to new concepts and commit to change, you will get something out of this book.

LAST CHANCE

If you are the type of person who believes the world is out to get you. If you get your feelings hurt if you aren't receiving constant accolades, praise, and attention. If you believe that you are being bullied because someone gave you constructive feedback, told you no, or told you off (which you probably deserved). If you are a notorious complainer filing grievances, engaging in social-media rants, sending lengthy invidious emails to recipients sure to spark resentment versus resolution. If you withdraw, call out sick, or go on medical leave after you get a poor performance review, even though deep down you know you did not perform excellently, you are an entitled and disempowered brat.

I have two things to say to you. First, get a freakin' life already. Second, this book is not for you. Ok, let me revise number two. Number one still stands. Actually, this book is for you, however I'm afraid that if you read it, you might sue me for emotional distress. So caution, read this book only if you are ready to take control of your life and have fully read and signed the waiver on the next page.

I, the willing reader of this book, hereby accept all risks to my feelings and my ego getting bruised or wounded that might result from the book. I hereby release author Lori Gentles from any and all liability to me, my personal representatives, estate, heirs, next of kin, and assigns for any and all claims and causes of action for temporary pain, discomfort, or metamorphosis to my person, that might result from or occur during my reading of the book.

I understand that this book will discuss adult topics related to personal and professional growth. The author will also occasionally use adult or profane language to emphasize a point or connect with or surprise the audience. Readers who are uncomfortable with such topics or language should not read this book.

Do you understand?

Signature _____ Date _____

Adapted from Darren Hardy HPF 2019.

You see, up until now, if you reacted to the situations I just described, you've been letting someone else control your life and then blaming them for your lack of happiness, health, wealth, love, and god knows what else. You know what you are or have become? A victim. Victims continue to be victimized at every turn in life. In the words of POTUS 45—"Sad! So sad!"

I have heard that the best books, movies, and stories are those that cause you to experience a range of emotions. This book will make you laugh, make you angry, piss you off, make you twitch in discomfort, and you might even cry once you realize how long you've suppressed your greatness. My goal is to inspire you, give you hope, activate your power of iChoice, and help you achieve your freedom, which is priceless. At the end of the day, I want you to be a better version of yourself, and I want to be a better version of myself. I, after all, am my first student.

SUMMARY

This is a book about making better choices, but more specifically about self-leadership and self-empowerment in all aspects of your personal and professional life. It is about choosing to go through a personal transformation and ridding yourself of a prevailing and unrealistic notion that responsibility for your happiness rests with someone other than you.

The desired outcome is to help you shift your mindset toward total personal responsibility and away from victimhood and entitlement. It really is all about you, your thinking, your choice, and your dreams. If you have been stuck in a victim mindset, overreliant on others for your joy and fulfillment, this book will completely and utterly awaken you to a new way of thinking.

For ease of reading, this book is divided into three parts.

Part 1: Your Personal Life—It All Starts with You

Change happens in a moment. The moment you decide, transformation occurs. It might take reality time to catch up, but the deed is done. Nothing is going to change for you until you change.

Part 2: Your Work Life—Understand the Contract

Simply put, no matter what situation you are in, there is a written or unwritten contract with specific terms. To succeed, you must understand and exceed the terms. If you don't like the terms, renegotiate or get out. It's your choice.

Part 3: Your Future Life—Don't Ask, Just Do!

You don't need permission to create the future you desire. Just do it. Stop waiting. Time is passing you by. No more excuses.

PART 1:

· ·

Your Personal Life—
It All Starts with You

CHAPTER 1

It's Up to You, Boo!

You're still here? Excellent. Let's get started. Here's a quiz. If you pass this, then and only then, can you proceed. Take a deep breath. Ready? Ok.

1. Do you believe or are you seeking to believe that you are in control of your life?

2. Do you believe or are you seeking to believe that you are 100 percent responsible for everything that happens in your life?

3. Do you believe or are you seeking to believe that you have the power to create a prosperous, happy, and healthy future?

4. Do you believe or are you seeking to believe that no matter what has happened in your personal or professional life, you can turn the tide starting right now?

5. Do you believe or are you seeking to believe that you were born with greatness and a purpose that only you are uniquely qualified to carry out?

6. Are you *not* completely happy with your life as it is and would you like help in changing your course?

If you answered yes to all these questions, congratulations. You may proceed. If you didn't, you have two choices. Either keep reading at your own risk and be open to the message, or put the book down now and continue with your life as it is.

You have a problem. You are living in agony and you might not even know it. You think it's normal, but it's not. Deep down inside, you want to be free. Free of chaos, free of conflict, free of depression and frustration, but you keep bringing yourself the same set of circumstances that actually creates the agony. I'm officially here to diagnose you as insane. No, I am not a psychologist or psychiatrist, but I know that if you keep doing the same thing over and over again and expect either different results or the same results, you have a problem. This is illogical and foolish behavior. Yet we do it anyway.

Ever wonder why it seems that everywhere you go, every job you have, every boss you work for, every church you attend, every teacher you've ever had, you experience the same problems. Your friends and family, those who have stuck around for the ride—bless their hearts—listen to you year after year griping and complaining about how unfair and difficult everything is. They don't have the heart or maybe even the awareness to tell you that um—it's you.

Hello, stop and look around. What is the common denominator in this equation? In all the circumstances you label as unfair—who is the one person always present? It's you, Boo. No, you are not unlucky, you are just dragging your baggage with you. As painful as this might be, it is the truth. Ever heard of the saying, "Wherever I go, there I am"? You can't escape you. This means that you are taking your garbage with you everywhere you go.

I had to come to this harsh reality myself. I still struggle with it from time to time. The reason is because I had a limiting belief that life was a struggle and that relationships—personal or professional—were hard. I believed that the world was inherently unfair and that people in general could not be trusted. Guess what? Because of this limiting belief, everything was hard and people were untrustworthy. I didn't know I was I prophet, a magician, a wizard. I didn't know that Murphy (creator of Murphy's Law where everything that can go wrong will go wrong) was my cousin. Everything I spoke happened.

I finally had to ask, "Is it me, or is it them?" Because I am not insane—I am open to self-reflection and betterment—I finally came to the conclusion that the source of my struggle was me and my beliefs and not every living thing that I came across. I could no longer blame the dog, my boss, or my team. The solution? Change my belief. This is not as easy as it sounds, mostly because we are lazy human beings. Although we might be discontent with the status quo, the effort to change it requires work and the status quo trumps effort.

Don't believe me? How many of you are discontent with that ten extra pounds you've been carrying around? How many of you are discontent with your anemic bank balance and skinny paycheck? How many of you are putting in the effort to change it? Boom. I rest my case.

But wait, there is hope. I know it would be so much easier to continue to blame all the people who crossed my path for everything wrong in my life and remain in a state of agony. But again, that would make me insane and a narcissist. Please, don't let me be insane.

So now that we've established that the problem is me—or in your case, you—what can you do about it? How can you stop the agony and be free?

THE SIX STEPS OF ESCAPING MENTAL AGONY THAT COME WITH INDECISION

Here is the formula that worked and is working for me.

Step One: Recognize Your Agony

Agony is a misalignment between your spirit and your ego. It is cognitive dissonance from where you are and where you want to be. It is a change in the terms of the contract you engaged in and the experience you are having. Every relationship is a contract with terms. You give of your time, talent, love, and money in exchange for recognition, a paycheck, a marriage proposal, or a burger.

Awareness is the first step in everything. Call it like it is. Don't rationalize the state you are in. Pain is a human experience, and unless you're an android, you will feel it. The human experience is necessary for you to know the spirit experience. The spirit experience (peace, calm, joy, freedom) is much better. The key is to move through the human experience, which is largely governed by our egos, as fast as possible.

Alcoholics can't say, "I drink too much." They must say, "I am an alcoholic." One frame will trick them into thinking they can handle it if they just drank a little bit less. The other frame says they can't drink at all. A person in agony must label it as such, any other label will trick him or her into thinking that this state of misery is normal thought processing.

The telltale signs of agony are doubt, confusion, uncertainty, and procrastination. The outcome is pain, frustration, entitlement, negativity, and delayed dreams. Agony doesn't have to be about something grand. You can be in agony over the most benign of things, such as the following.

Should I eat that donut?

Should I quit my job?

Should I go out with this person?

Should I send that email?

When you begin a statement with *should*, you are in a state of agony. An insidious cousin of should is maybe.

I know I am a diabetic, but maybe it's ok if I eat this donut.

Maybe I should quit my job.

I know he's not exactly what I want, but maybe he will change.

Should and maybe are signs of doubt. You only ask these questions because you are in conflict with what you might want to do and what you know to do. The answer is always within you, but you ask these questions which allow you to talk yourself out of what you already know to do. The answer is usually the opposite of what you are asking and agonizing over.

Step Two: Decide to Change

There is no magic to deciding, but there is a process. It is different from trying. It is different from wanting and wishing. You always have a backdoor escape hatch when you *try* to do

something. And most people will use it at the first sign of difficulty, abandoning their goal. They give up or give in when they
don't see immediate results or they have a bad day.

Deciding is not a physical action, it is a spiritual action.
You first get into agreement with your spiritual purpose.
Understanding your spiritual purpose is simple but not necessarily easy. If you are unhappy and discontent with your life
most of the time, my guess is that you are not operating in
your spiritual purpose. Behavioral therapists call this cognitive dissonance. Much of our pain comes from misalignment.
When you become aware of this, decisions become less about
deciding and more about *listening* and *choosing* the path that is
most aligned.

One way to listen to your spirit is through meditation. A lot of
people shy away from meditation because they believe it is some
foo-foo activity reserved for hippies, weirdos, and barefooted,
tree-hugging people. No shade. I possess many of these traits.

Actually, meditation is just asking yourself a question, like
"What do I really want to do?" Then just sit quietly for five
minutes—or for as long as you want or can—and wait for the
answer. I have learned that if I am agonizing over a decision to
do or to not do something, and the answer isn't an immediate
and resounding yes, then it is a no.

Agony is pain, and pain means misalignment. That inbetween
state of maybe or exerting energy trying to convince yourself
that you should do a certain thing is exhausting and anxiety
laden. There is an instant relief once you make a decision that
aligns with your spirit. You are mentally free. True freedom is
mental freedom. Exhale.

Think back to a time when you were stressed over a decision and once you made it you felt instant relief.

What was your internal conversation?

_____
_____
_____
_____

How did you get to the decision point?

_____
_____
_____
_____

What is a decision you are struggling with now that is caus-ing you pain?

_____
_____
_____
_____

What is influencing your internal dialogue (others' opinions, societal expectations, your pride, your ego, etc.)?

_____
_____
_____
_____

What is your gut (that is, your spirit) telling you?

_____

_____

_____

· · · · · · · · · · · · · **TIP:** · · · · · · · · · · · · ·

The answer is in the struggle.
The decision you are agonizing over is the no.

For example, I recall a time when I moved from my home-town to take a lucrative job in another state. I had been gone for at least five years and my family and friends wanted me to come back home. Finally, an opportunity presented itself that could take me home. An offer was on the table. I called my sister and a close friend at least three times in one night to ask what I should do. Should I take the job?

Finally, my friend, in her wisdom, said, and probably because she was sick of me calling her, "You know the answer already. If you really wanted to take the job, you wouldn't be asking me. The fact that you are agonizing over the decision means it's not time yet." That message was profound. I did not take the job. Once I called the recruiter to decline the offer, I felt instant relief. Aah, alignment.

Step Three: Declare the Decision *in the* Affirmative

When I decided to decline the offer, instead of declaring, "I am not going to take the job," I said, "I am going to keep the job I have." Stating decisions in the affirmative reinforces a position of strength, power, choice, and spiritual alignment. The opposite approach, saying that I turned down, rejected, or declined the offer causes self-doubt, regret, and unnecessary questions and skepticism from others.

People will undoubtedly ask, "Why did you turn down the job?" This puts you on the defensive and causes you to doubt or defend your decision. Stating your decision in the affirmative is a subtle but profound modification that infuses you with confidence. People will want to celebrate with you for your intelligent choice versus question you about the choice you rejected.

Step Four: Check your Gut

Once you've made a decision and declared it in the affirmative, do a gut check. Ask, "Do I feel like a weight has been lifted? Am I at peace with my decision? Do I feel relieved?"

We've all had experiences where we felt obligated to attend a social event. We didn't want to go and dreaded the notion of it. We start an internal dialogue trying to convince ourselves to do something we truly don't want to do out of fear of being labeled antisocial. "I don't want to go but *maybe* I *should*." Those are two dangerous words that indicate mental agony. At some point, we affirmatively decide to stay home. We get a moment of clarity. Once we make the decision, we feel instant relief.

Whether you're in mental agony about whether to attend a social event, end an unhealthy relationship, quit a toxic job, or eat the donut, once you make the decision that aligns with your spirit, you will breathe a sigh of relief.

Take a moment and think about a time when you experienced mental agony caused by indecision.

How did you get to the decision point?

_____

_____

_____

_____

_____

Did you know the answer all along?

_____

_____

_____

_____

Step Five: Repeat ad nauseam

Practice makes perfect. Sage advice we learned as kids. Any new behavior requires practice. You will have to develop muscle memory for this new approach. As stated previously, it is simple but not necessarily easy. You are a spirit being having a human experience. You will have to go against your natural human tendency to get off the road most traveled.

Step Six: Be Free

You are what you say you are. Claim it. Say, "I am free—free from stress, anxiety, and confusion." These steps will imbue confidence, empowerment, and strength. Each decision made that aligns with your spirit gets you closer to freedom. These micro-moments of freedom compounded over time will lead to your ultimate freedom.

The number one thing people most want in the world is freedom. No one wants to be bound by societal pressures and made to feel guilty because of the shoulda, coulda, woulda. We all want financial, physical, and mental freedom. These six steps will help you get on this path.

CHAPTER 2

Whatcha Gonna Do Now?

Is this too real for you? My goal is to jolt you into a state of awareness. It is the first step. But awareness, like knowledge, is nothing unless you accept it and apply it. Not only do you need to be aware that you *might* be the problem, you have to accept the fact that you *are* the problem.

Acceptance is the next step. You have to get to the point where you admit that you are 100 percent responsible for the experiences in your life. Whoa, wait one second. You can't be serious? I'll accept responsibility for some things but come on. How can I be 100 percent responsible for experiences in my life? This is a ridiculous notion.

Calm down. I know how you feel. When someone first told me this, I flat out rejected it. I thought it utterly absurd, and I just couldn't believe it. I didn't want to believe it. It took me a long time to embrace this concept, and, truth be told, sometimes I regress to self-preservation through blaming others for my experiences.

Thankfully, I've learned to recognize the signs of self-pity and victimhood, and I quickly change my state of being by taking ownership of myself, my feelings, and my response to circumstances. If only I had learned these concepts earlier in life. I would have saved myself from wasted time and delayed dreams. I don't want your dreams to be delayed. So, to help you embrace this concept faster, so that you can get on with life, for god's sake, let me explain what it means to be 100 percent responsible for the experiences in your life.

First, let's be clear, it does not mean that you literally are responsible for creating or causing tragedy, pain, or heartbreak. Although you do play a role in creating certain conditions based on your energy and beliefs, I would be hard-pressed to say that you singlehandedly caused the wildfire that destroyed your home (this actually happened to me), or that you created the six-car pileup that killed multiple people including children, or that you caused the economic collapse that resulted in high unemployment. Of course not.

However, what it means is that shit happens. Events in life, for the most part, are just events. Please stay with me. This is where I'm bound to lose someone. Even the car crash where several people were injured and died is an event. Believe it or not, some people will interpret that event in a positive light and some will interpret it in a negative light. Ever wonder why that is. Is everyone's opinion wrong and yours the only right one?

If you take the position that your belief is right and another person's perspective is wrong, what does this make you? A narcissist—I know, I'm obsessed with this word. Interpretation is based on individual beliefs, your spiritual upbringing, and all of your experiences. Our interpretation of things determines the meaning of that thing. Much has been written on this subject and it is too deep and cerebral to go into here and it's not my area of expertise.

Let me just say this, the bottom line is that you get to choose how you will interpret various events that occur in your life. Romans 8:28, King James Version, says that "All things work together for good to them that love God, to them who are the called according to his purpose." Some choose to believe that this Bible verse means that even those things that people typically interpret as bad somehow will work out for the greater good. I happen to fully believe this. My perspective is a choice and a positive perspective, even in the wake of what doesn't feel good, it is a gift.

To illustrate this point, I'll share a parable about a farmer and his neighbor.

> *A farmer has a horse that runs away. The neighbor says, "Oh, how unfortunate, such bad news." The farmer replies, "Who's to say if this is good or bad?" The next day, the horse returns with a few wild horses. The neighbor says, "Congratulations, such good fortune— good news." The farmer replies, "Who's to say if this is good or bad?" The farmer's son decides to mount a wild horse and is thrown off and breaks his leg. The neighbor says, "Oh, no, what bad luck—so sad." The farmer replies, "Who's to say if this is good or bad?" Shortly thereafter, the government is recruiting every appropriate male to fight in a war. The farmer's son was exempted because of his broken leg.*

If we look closely and examine experiences with an open mind, we will see that events in our lives come to serve us. We can't always see it in the moment of pain and heartache. We have to train our brains to reinterpret events. And as crazy as it seems, the bottom line is that we can't experience joy without sorrow, laughter without tears, and happiness without sadness. We must experience the polar opposite.

When my house burned down in one of the largest California wildfires to date, I lost everything, except for my pets and the clothes on my back. Everyone expected me to crumble. My friends and coworkers believed I was in a state of shock and in denial because I maintained an upbeat and positive attitude. They told me, "You should seek counseling; it's going to hit you later. You are going to experience extreme sadness and depression." I assured everyone that I was fine.

Although there were moments of sadness—mostly when I let my mind spin around what could've happened (I could have died if I didn't make it out of the house in time). Aside from the what-if scenarios, I was more than fine. I felt free. I couldn't share my little secret, because it was so counter to what was expected of me.

I felt free because I was alive and I could have easily died.

I felt free because I knew that the slate had been cleared for something new.

I felt free because I got to see and experience the kindness of strangers, which renewed my faith in humankind.

I felt free because my faith was being tested and I passed the test.

Can you imagine the power you would have if you could garner this truth and leverage every situation presented to you for your greater good? How differently would you handle the shit that just keeps happening? You don't have to lose all material things to do this. You can leverage the experiences at work with that horrible boss who undermines your authority, the unnecessarily hostile and rude customer service representative, the derogatory comment, or a gesture received from a stranger for no reason at all.

Stop for a moment. Think about something that happened to you that you labeled as bad in the moment. Can you identify at least three positive things that came out of the situation?

Describe the Situation: _____

1.

_____

_____

_____

2.

_____

_____

_____

3.

_____

_____

_____

There are different versions of the farmer story. The moral of the story, regardless of version, is that things just happen in life. We get to choose how we interpret the situations. When we judge events as bad, they are bad. When we examine the situation and look for its grander meaning, we discover unexpected insight.

You are in control of your emotions and your feelings. No one can make you happy, mad, sad, or angry. You get happy, mad, sad, or angry based on your interpretation of the originating event. Your feelings are not wrong. And if you don't like the way you feel, if you are in pain, you can change.

You choose. You always choose, even when you think things are thrust on you. You choose your response.

Ok, time to check in with you. How are you feeling right now? Are you irritated? Do you think this is bullshit and that I just don't understand your circumstances? Are you ready to burn the book? If so, ask yourself why. Examine your emotions. I don't control you, so I can't make you feel anything. You feel a certain way because of your interpretation of an experience.

Perhaps it could be that I've uprooted an issue that needs further exploration. Great! Exploration leads to growth.

Are you ready for growth? Are you ready to take full responsibility for your experiences in life? If so, here's what you can do now. Repeat the following mantra:

iChoose to see events that occur in my life as happening *for* me, not *to* me.

iChoose to challenge the interpretation of events and ask myself what is causing me to react in a certain way.

iChoose to accept that my emotions and feelings are mine and mine alone; no one can make me feel a certain way.

iChoose to change my experience by changing my interpretations, emotions, and feelings if they are not serving me.

iChoose to take full responsibility for my health, happiness, and wellness.

iChoose to forgive myself for blaming others for my failings

Lynn G. Robbins, cofounder of FranklinCovey, gave a speech about being "100 percent responsible" for all parts of our lives. He said that being responsible "is to recognize ourselves as being the cause for the effects or results of our choices—good or bad." He identifies the anti-responsible person as blaming others, making excuses, etc. This is extremely dangerous, but he says that so many people default to the anti-responsible approach as a defense mechanism to avoid shame, embarrassment, stress, anxiety, and the pain and negative consequences of mistakes.

If you could kick the person in the pants responsible for most of your trouble, you wouldn't sit for a month.

—Theodore Roosevelt

CHAPTER 3

Mind Your Damn Business

can't tell you how many times I made a decision to change my life. Got all pumped up and righteously declared that this was it. I would transform my thick thighs into lean, strong sexy specimens. I would return to my too-underweight-to-donate-blood poundage. I would finish the book I've been working on since the turn of the century. I would, I would, I would—fill in the blank.

Time after time, my declarations coupled with my determination got me to first base. First base is good, but at some point, I needed to cross home plate. I always seemed to strike out before I made it to home base. I don't really know sports analogies but I think you get my point.

What's the problem? The problem is that I lose sight of the goal. I get distracted, I am overtaken by the three Ds. I allow my vision toward betterment to *drift* away (first D) with shifting winds and tides, to *drown* under competing pressures (second D), or I remain in a *dream* state (third D) fantasizing about a better future. If I'm honest with myself, minding someone else's business instead of my own simply distracts me.

I mind the refrigerator; I mind Netflix; I mind irritating people; I mind Twitter rants and every other ridiculous stimulus that does not serve my mission or me. Forget the Kardashians. Dare I say that I'm distracted by Kanye, the ridiculous housewives of wherever, and scandals of the rich and foolish? I mind everything except my own damn business.

My distractions are insidiously and cleverly disguised as progress, effort, and productivity. Instead of actually sitting down to write my book, I convince myself that reading some-one else's book is research that will help me with my book. Or, before I actually work out, I convince myself that rest is also a form of self-care—so I will just rest tonight and work out tomorrow. Sly devil! I have spent countless hours, days, and years planning, researching, and studying only to find myself bookless with thick thighs.

Don't mistake activity for action or progress. Activity without focus is regression, not progression.

Admittedly this might take time to embrace and adopt. We don't like liars, but we lie to ourselves all the time and cover it up with more lies called rationalizations. Let's break this down. Rationalize is to tell a rational lie. I've been lying to myself for years. One of my biggest lies is that I deserve to binge on Netflix for hours a day because my mind needs a break . . . Come on, Lori! Really? For years I have tried to curb this distraction (aka addiction). I *rational lied* myself into thinking that I could limit myself to one or two episodes a night. Have you tried eating one Hershey's Kisses or one potato chip—especially the wavy kind? It can't be done, people.

Finally, after many years, mind you, I just gave up Netflix, cold turkey. I came home one day disgusted with myself having made little progress on my passion and prosperity projects the weekend prior. I had wasted time on Netflix's business instead of my own. The people who acted in, produced, or were featured in the shows were fulfilling their dreams while I mindlessly delayed mine. Oh slap! Twice. Wake up, girl! Oh yeah, my decision to go cold turkey is saving me $8.99 a month. That's $107.88 a year. I only need $999,892.20 more dollahs to make millionaire status. Ooh, ooh!

Minding your own business requires you to become self-centered. Self-centeredness is typically used in derogatory terms but not here. When it comes to achieving your goals, you must focus on self. Don't confuse this with being selfish. No one likes a selfish, inconsiderate, entitled brat. Get rid of those bastards. Self-centered in this instance means focusing on what *you* do—not on what others do.

You constantly compete against your own best self and measure your progress against your status of yesterday. Are you better today than you were yesterday?

Forget about what others are doing. The only time you should focus on what others are doing is for an inspirational boost. For example, when I'm hiking a steep mountain, and I'm tired and really want to quit, I see someone much older or seemingly less in shape than me facing the challenge head-on. They inspire me to keep moving. I don't try to catch up with them or pass them. But they give me the boost of inspiration that I need to keep going—at my own pace. The key is that I keep moving. The added benefit is that someone will see me continuing to move forward and also be inspired.

Unfortunately, there are the Suspicious Sallys and Doubting Daniels of the world. These fools spend all their time comparing themselves to others. These are the people who always keep score. They don't want anyone to get ahead or get one thing more than they have. Never mind that others put in the work to earn it.

Ironically, the Suspicious Sallys and Doubting Daniels are not stupid people. They are typically smart but lack self-awareness. They somehow feel entitled and powerless. They don't realize that if they just focused on themselves and their goals instead of measuring themselves against others, they would be further ahead. They choose to stay stuck in the slow lane. They don't want anyone to pass them, and they won't pass anyone. They complain about the status quo but have settled nicely into it. They are comfortable in their discomfort.

Mind your damn business, Sally and Daniel. Don't you understand that you have the power to create a different and prosperous reality? In fact, the prosperity and abundance has always existed, but the Sallys and Daniels can't see it. Some people can't see what's right in front of them or what's rightfully theirs, because they are so entrenched in guarding, cultivating, and nurturing their FBS—faulty belief system. Our BS, largely developed as children, is often faulty.

Almost all behavior is driven by our subconscious brain, which runs on FBS. Our FBS is so powerful it allows us to irrationally justify, defend, protect, oddly love, and accept our self-imposed misery and discomfort. Take for example, Suspicious Sally and Doubting Daniel. They hate their jobs but stay because they believe that most people hate their jobs. They believe that being miserable is just part of the plan. They believe that suffering every day to get employment benefits and a paycheck is the tradeoff and that there are no other options but this reality.

Sally and Daniel think little of their lives. They choose to waste their precious time, aging and letting time pass them by, while complaining the entire time. What a miserable existence. I'm not sure if I would be writing this book with such passion if it weren't for the complainers I've met throughout my career.

It is so hard for me to understand this mindset, but the truth is we have all been Sally or Daniel at some point. I got fed up being Sally. I want to live as me—Lori—that means victorious. Sally and Daniel irritate the hell out of me. And I want to help them change. I can help them change. Sometimes I want to slap the Sallys and the Daniels out of their stupor. But last time I checked that would be considered assault. Writing this book is a healthier outlet, and I get to stay out of jail.

CHAPTER 4

Get Off Your Big Fat But[t]

Sally's got a big ole butt. Say what! Daniel's got a big ole butt. That's right. Yep, you got a big ole butt. *But* that is. Your *but* is getting bigger. I don't mean your toosh, your derrière, your arse. Although based on the obesity epidemic in America, your actual butt is likely bigger too. I'd bet a Big Mac on it. As the ridiculously ripped, tall, dark, and handsome trainer said, in a matter-of-fact way when I asked him for tips on how to lose my back fat, "Stay out of the kitchen." No ifs, ands, or buts. Umm hmm, thank you for that profound advice genius (lip smack—eye roll).

In the previous chapter, I mentioned the refrigerator as one of my distractions—so I know he's on to something. His response was still annoying.

Light bulb: When people tell you the truth—sometimes it is annoying and painful.

It's like Listerine mouthwash—when it burns, it's working. What he was really trying to say is for me to stop making excuses for my back fat. Stop trying to find an alternative remedy to fix a problem when I can address the root of the problem. Take action or change my actions that got me the back fat. Don't fight the pain (truth)—embrace it.

The word *but* is used a million times every day to *ratio-nal-lies* our dumb and tired excuses. Your fat *but* is the enemy of your success. Like Pinocchio's nose that grew every time he told a lie, every time you use *but*, it grows. You think you are lying or deceiving others, but to be honest, most people don't care about what you are doing. They only genuinely care if it affects them in some way. But you should care. You are only cheating yourself.

It doesn't matter what comes after "but" — all that matters is that it stops you from accomplishing something.
—Katie Berbert

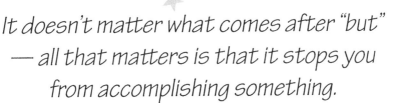

Many articles have been written on the dangers of using the word *but* You must get it out of your vocabulary and here are the three reasons why you must do so immediately if you want to see results and change your life.

1. **You are a victor instead of a victim.** Say it with me. "I am not a victim." When you use the word *but* before anything to explain why you did or didn't do something, you are relegating yourself to the hood—Victimhood, that is. Who do you know that wants to live in Victimhood on purpose? I think most people would choose to live in Victorhill if they believed it was possible.

2. **You are intelligent and powerful.** Using *but* to explain away a decision you made is lame and makes you sound unintelligent and disempowered. You're a smart, responsible person. Own your actions and decisions. Don't try to excuse them away. Acknowledge that you simply did or did not do something and commit to making it right by . . . you got it . . . just doing it—whatever *it* is.

3. **You are strong and empowered.** Excuses are useless and are tricks for kids. But the dog ate it. But I didn't know what to do. But no one told me. But I didn't know I could. But disempowers you. You give your power away in exchange for holding on to your big fat *but*. Foolishly, people think the *but* protects them or gives them a pass. There might be plenty of reasons why something did or did not happen. That does not mean you shouldn't take total personal responsibility, right? No free passes here.

The solution to a big and growing *but* is to do what you say, say what you mean, follow up, follow through, and anticipate consequences. Simple. People would be further ahead if they mastered this basic posture.

Are you ready to lose your fat *but*? Practice this daily mantra with conviction.

iChoose to live in Victorhill versus Victimhood.

iChoose to make intelligent choices versus excuses.

iChoose mature actions over childlike behavior.

iChoose total personal responsibility (TPR) over blaming.

iChoose to lose my big fat *but* and exercise new empowering behaviors daily.

Billions of people have passed through this planet and never realized their greatness and never achieved their dreams. Why? They didn't have the guts to risk the life they were living for the one they were capable of.

—Darren Hardy

CHAPTER 5

Embrace Your Power

The killer of success is defensiveness, competition, and suspicion. Imagine if we shifted from competition to cooperation and creativity. We could solve problems more readily and achieve exponential gains. We would be free to share our knowledge without fear of losing our power. We would stop living like prehistoric people in constant fight-or-flight mode, believing in scarcity versus abundance.

We are in the modern age and each of us individually can do something to help elevate someone else. There is more than enough of everything to go around. Believing otherwise subscribes to the faulty and limiting theory of scarcity. And because we get what we believe (self-fulfilling prophecy) it further cements our faulty belief. We wonder why we keep experiencing the same results. The answer is simple.

You create it. What you hold in your head can be held in your hand. What you think and believe becomes tangible. As much as you'd like to make an excuse and blame others for your outcomes, the reality is that it's you. Painful but true. A person with total personal responsibility (TPR) will embrace this and feel empowered to create a new and better reality. Darren Hardy, author and self-improvement mentor, says that every outcome in your life has been created in one of three ways.

1. By What You Did

The good, the bad, and the ugly. Stop making excuses. Yes, there might be good reasons why you did something, but reasons are excuses in drag.

2. By What You Didn't Do but Knew You Could Have, Should Have, and Didn't

People complain about all sorts of things—processes, rules (many self-imposed rules that could easily be changed), events, relationships, and their weight. Chronic complainers, when asked what they've done to improve the situation, usually come up with an excuse for their lack of action. They blame the system, their upbringing, their boss, or the secret ingredient in their favorite unhealthy snack. The default to blame negates their power.

3. By How You Responded to What Happened

You have total control over how you react to everything. Your interpretation of an event plays a key role. Let's acknowledge that some things in life suck, are hard, or frustrating. The key is to reframe disempowering situations into empowering ones by tapping in to your inner strength and leveraging the situation at hand for your greater good.

We've been bamboozled and snookered into believing that other people are responsible for our outcomes. Contemporary literature on leadership perpetuates this, which spurs on the pervasiveness of entitlement. If you work a day job, you might feel that it is the supervisor's responsibility to invest in your future. Of course, any employer will want to invest in its most valuable asset. **Real growth happens when you choose to invest in yourself.**

You can give yourself more of what you need in terms of self-validation, care, love, and promotion than anyone can. Stop waiting on others to affirm you. Affirm yourself first and akin to the *Field of Dreams*, others will affirm you too. It happens in that order. To be fully empowered is to recognize that no one is responsible for you. Waiting on others puts you in a state of perpetual disappointment, powerless to make others do what you want them to do. To the contrary, if you are disappointed with yourself, you can give yourself a sobering slap to get yourself in gear.

A friend and colleague with a six-figure income didn't think he was worth $300. He thought that the company he worked for should think he was worth $300 and invest it by sending him to a three-day transformative learning experience. He missed out on a lifechanging opportunity waiting on his boss to pay. This is the epitome of disempowerment. The value gained from the training would far exceed the $300 that he spent in one month on fancy coffee drinks and unhealthy lunches.

Knowledge is like a giving tree. The confidence and strength gained through knowledge is priceless and its application endless. Sadly, most people, like my colleague, think small and make small investments in things with diminishing or zero returns. Gary Vaynerchuck of VaynerMedia said on an Instagram post, "Stop buying dumb shit." He was referring to investing in things that don't advance your mission. To expound on his in-your-face message, stop buying into dumb lies, dumb beliefs, and dumb people who tell you lies. This is raw but real.

Fear gets in the way of you embracing your power. Fear causes you to buy into dumb shit. Fear is false evidence appearing real. The way to eliminate the fear of failure, rejection, defeat, or overwhelming success is to put your ego aside. Ego gets in the way of you doing what you need to do to achieve your dreams.

Stop caring so much about what people think.

Here's a little secret that's not so secret—people really aren't thinking about you as much as you think they are. In the words of a Jay-Z song, "I got 99 problems, but a b**ch ain't one." You're the one thinking about them, thinking about you, which they are not. Get it. Ridiculous, right? You're focusing on the wrong things and playing too small. You were not designed to be small but to be a giant. Stop squandering your time and talent.

I had a colleague bent out of shape and giving me the cold shoulder over an email mishap. She interpreted my response to an email that was addressed to both of us as me not needing her help. She informed me that I should have told her that I was going to respond—mind you, she didn't inform me that she was taking care of the situation. In short, her feelings were hurt and she felt devalued. So, I apologized, reassured her that I did need her help and explained why I responded to an email that was addressed to me.

She, on the other hand, chose not to acknowledge her role in the situation and remained bent out of shape over the incident. She did not take responsibility or control over her actions when she could have. If she did, the outcome would have been vastly different. Instead, she opted to blame. She failed to realize that my actions didn't cause her to feel a certain way. She felt a certain way because she chose to interpret the situation in a disempowering fashion. Her ego was in control.

My goal is to strengthen the constitution of everyone so that they are solid in their identity; confident in their knowledge, value, and contribution; mature in their response; and able to recognize, own, and redirect negative emotions that are created by themselves into something positive. It didn't work with her, but I trust it will work with you.

As we end Part 1, commit to not making excuses. Stop complaining and replace it with creating—creating a more prosperous and successful future.

PART 2:

....

Your Work Life— Understand the Contract

CHAPTER 6

Conspiracy Theory

All right, now that you have your house in order, you can focus on your work situation. If you don't work in the traditional sense of working for a company, substitute work for wherever you are in life. Your situation might be as volunteer, student, parent, spouse, or prisoner. Prisoner? Really? Hey, I don't know your life! You might be incarcerated reading this book. That would be really awesome—not the jail part, of course (unless you're a rapist or a serial killer; then I kinda think you need to be in jail—I'm just sayin')—but the fact you're reading this book is awesome. In fact, if you are in jail, you likely got there because of the choices you made based on your beliefs about you.

The good news is that wherever you are, you can free yourself. Viktor E. Frankl said in his book, *Man's Search for Meaning*, "Everything can be taken from a man but one thing: the last of human freedoms—to choose one's attitude in any given set of circumstances, to choose one's own way." As stated before, you always have choice and everything you do is based on a choice you made, even when you think someone else is to blame.

This faulty thinking is straight from the hood—Victimhood, that is. Remember that neighborhood? I've never met so many people in the workplace who live in the same neighborhood. Pay and benefits are good, working conditions pleasant, opportunity and upward mobility abound, you would think that more people would choose to move on up to the East Side to finally get a piece of the pie . . . otherwise known as Victorhill. But nope. Incredulous!

I just can't understand or believe that people deliberately choose to live in Victimhood when presented with a clear way out. My theory (I need to find some way to explain this phenomenon because it's driving me crazy) is that people sub-scribe to the People's Plan.

The People's Plan is a scam. It's worse than a pyramid scheme; it's worse than identity theft. Come to think of it, it is identity theft. The People's Plan, if you buy in to it, will absolutely rob you of your identity. Reclaiming your identity will be exceedingly difficult. LifeLock theft protection will not be able to help you. Not only is your identity stolen but your soul is sold. The People's Plan seduces you with a promise of prosperity, hope, success, freedom, and hap-piness. Once you are hooked, the plan traps you using fear tactics. The results are the following.

You keep working every day at a job you no longer like, with people you can't stand, for money that's not enough for the effort, for far too many years, with a small glimmer of hope toward retirement, and a pension inadequate even for a non-luxury lifestyle. Forget about vacationing during your golden years. You need every cent to pay rent and afford your weekly grocery shopping spree at the discount grocery store.

Nevertheless, people keep subscribing to the People's Plan and continue to tolerate its miserable promise of barely enough.

I'm amazed at what people tolerate. Tolerations are the tools of the disempowered. Empowered people don't tolerate shit. Why? They know they don't have to. They know they have choice. They know that life is what they make it, not what others dish out. They know they can't control other people, but they absolutely know that they can control their reactions and responses to other peo-ple. They ultimately know that there is a better plan.

Yep, there is better plan. You've got it; it's called the Prosperous People's Plan (PPP).

Unlike the seduction of the People's Plan scam and the bait-and-switch method, when you subscribe to PPP, you choose to trade your time doing something you dislike for something you actually love. You choose to create the spectacular life you desire instead of accepting a life like others. You choose to follow your dreams versus burying your dream for an inadequate paycheck and the feeling of disenfranchisement.

Notice a pattern? You choose. Say it out loud. Say, "I choose." No, don't just read the phrase. Pause from reading and say it out loud.

"I choose."

Just saying it makes you stand a little taller, feel a little stronger. As long as you live your life based on what someone else wants—someone else's choice for you—you will never be prosperous. When you live life for you, regardless of how much you earn, you will be prosperous. Prosperity, like beauty, is in the eye of the beholder. The funny thing is that, amazingly, when you are doing what you want to do and are successful at it, money will follow you.

Successful people don't follow money; money follows successful people.

I feel the need to clarify here so there is no confusion. Some people are really good at sitting on their booty—doing nothing but eating and watching TV. They are excellent at it. But make no mistake, no prosperity, no money, no success is coming their way. What is likely to come their way is obesity, depression, diabetes, poverty, and unhappiness.

Can you picture it? You sitting on the couch, eating powdered sugar donuts and a family-size package of salty barbeque potato chips, and drinking a supersized bottle of soda. You blaming the world for your woes, convinced of a conspiracy theory, that the world has it out for you. You convinced that your parents didn't give you a leg up in life. You thinking that your boss treated you unfairly and never gave you a chance. You honestly believe that the world has conspired against you because it wants you to be broke and tired.

Wake up, please (slap, slap; left cheek, right cheek). You are the conspiracy theorist. You've conspired against yourself. You are preventing your higher best self from shining. You think and speak of negativity, insecurity, inadequacy, and voila, it appears. Your beliefs bring about your reality.

You can always tell what a person truly believes by their results.

This is a harsh reality and most people prefer to stay in denial and believe the conspiracy. It's less painful. But now that you're awake after the double slap across your face, you can leverage your paranoia for your good by becoming an inverse paranoid maniac.

Act and believe as if the world is conspiring to help you.

Instead of believing that everyone is using their precious time to plot and scheme against you, to trip you up, to obstruct your success, flip the script. Believe that everyone you come into contact with is instead rooting for you, cheering you on, and setting you up to win big. No matter where you go or what you do, you can't lose. Why? Because there is a conspiracy for your good.

What you imagine, visualize, and hold in your mind man-ifests. Thoughts become things. According to the universal law of cause and effect, your thoughts, behaviors, and actions create specific effects that manifest and create your life as you know it. Don't like the life you know? You can change it.

Visualize people around you responding enthusiastically and positively to your needs. People want to help and want to be needed. So, instead of preparing to defend yourself, putting on rejection repellent, gearing up for a fight, visualize people waiting eagerly to help you meet your goals. And let's just say by chance you become an inverse paranoid and there is that one miserable person who revels in other people's demise—so what.

Just say what the ole Southern Baptist church folk say, "I'm gonna pray for you, baby—you need Jesus." Come up with your own saying . . . but whatever you do, don't let one sick miserable mofo get in your way. Also, remember that even royal mofos are brilliant—they just don't know it yet.

Pray, chant, light a candle for enlightenment and keep moving forward. All good that you put out will come back to you. You reap what you sow—you know this—the other side of cause and effect.

CHAPTER 7

Yo Momma Don't Work Here

Let's get this straight. You are an adult; you are self-sufficient. You make choices every day—some good, some bad, some stupid. You do not rely on others to pave the way for you. Not your momma, your employer, your partner, or your coworker. Get it together. You are in charge of you. It is no one's job to motivate you. Motivate your own damn self. Better yet—get inspired.

Motivation is temporal. Inspiration comes from the inside, is self-replenishing, and can stand the test of time. When things get tough, if you are intrinsically inspired, you can generate your own energy to keep going. You won't have to rely on your boss to "motivate" you. A leader's job is to cultivate, not coddle. Coddling might be in the momma/child contract, but it is not in the employment contract—read the small print.

The traditional employee/employer relationship is lopsided. There is a disturbing and crippling misconception that the employer is supposed to make employees happy, promote them, understand their family needs, support them, not hurt their feelings, and give them fifty million chances, even though they are underperforming. Aargh!

I actually had an employee tell me that as the leader, I am responsible for their level of overall happiness on the job. I don't know about you, but I flat out reject this notion that I'm responsible for someone else's happiness. True, as a leader, there are certain responsibilities one has, such as cultivating a positive and safe work environment where individuals can flourish and grow. But to say anyone is responsible for your happiness is just too much. Make me happy, boss? Get real.

Unfortunately, contemporary literature on leadership endorses this unrealistic notion. I proclaim traditional leadership dead. Traditional leadership perpetuates mediocrity and entitlement; it undercuts creativity, ingenuity, and resiliency that is generated through self-reliance. Dependency on the supervisor (employer) for emotional and physical health, personal and professional happiness, and financial security is shortsighted. This mentality hurts organizations, hurts individuals, and dare I say hurts the nation.

If we really cared about people, we'd teach them to fish, to swim, to walk, to run, and to fly. We need to dare to care by telling people the truth with compassion. I'm worried that leading voices on leadership espousing a dysfunctional overreliance on the supervisor as superhero will systematically create a population of entitled brats and erode innovation.

The educational system and enabling parents are partly the cause. Yes, I'm talking to you, Mom and Dad, who want to make sure little Daniel has a better life than you. You allowed Daniel (who grows up to be Doubting Daniel) to go to school without completing his homework. You gave him a pass because you didn't want to interfere with his natural bio rhythm. WTF? Being modern parents and all, you support his school-home-play balance. Daniel showed up for class unprepared but no problem—he got an A for the day. It takes effort just to show up and that should count for something . . . Daniel thinks he's great!

Little Daniel is also on the soccer team. His team sucks, and he is a terrible player. That's ok though because everyone on the team, including Daniel—who never actually played a game and can't even kick the ball—will get a shiny trophy. Daniel thinks he's great. You, his parent, think this is ok because Daniel had fun and that's all that matters, right? Wrong.

First, let me say that Daniel is not great. Correction, he might have the ability to be great but he is not demonstrating greatness at the moment. Second, having fun matters but it's not all that matters. The ability to get things done also matters. Taking responsibility for your actions matter. Falling and getting back up and learning from your mistakes matter. Celebrating when you've truly earned the right to celebrate matters. I know, I know, you're just trying to build Daniel's little ego and increase his self-esteem.

The problem is that little egos in little people turn into big egos in big people and it is not cute. Daniel now works for me and in exactly three months he is looking for his first promotion, a raise, or to be named employee of the month. There are a million Daniels, and they all behave the same way. Why wouldn't they? They've experienced fake success and recognition their whole life. They think they are great when they are average at best.

We've created entitled and ungrateful takers. Always looking to get but not putting forth effort to earn the get. Wouldn't it be awesome if the employment contract included the following terms and conditions of employment? "Employee must be a grownup. Must not exhibit negative behaviors, including whining, blaming, complaining, bullying, subversion, or sabotage. Tantrums of any kind or demonstrations of the above-mentioned behaviors will result in immediate dismissal." This is my dream. But sadly, if employers took this approach to employment, they'd have no employees.

The best I can do at this time is to explain how the employee/employer contract works in hopes that the Daniels of the world will get with the program.

The Employee/Employer Contract

1. When you accept an employment position, you have entered into a *contract*. You exchange your talents, skills, knowledge, and abilities for money. You show up at the designated time, you do what you've agreed to do, and you get paid for services rendered.

2. The employer is not your family. There is no obligation for the employer to take care of you or your emotional needs. Your mother might play this role for you, but, hello, you are in the workplace and yo mamma don't work here. Repeat, the workplace is not a substitute for family.

EMPLOYEE CONTRACT TERMS

Employee **show up** for work **on time** –
do the work.

Employee continues to **grow** and **contribute** to the
success of the **organization**.

EMPLOYER CONTRACT TERMS

Employer **provide safe work environment –
pay fairly** for the work.

Employer **provide** developmental **opportunities** and
support continued growth.

I cringe when people refer to the workplace and coworkers as family. Please . . . you know you have crazy people in your family you don't want to be around but you feel obligated because of the "blood is thicker than water" thing and all. Well, there is no bloodline in the office, so cut it out, why don't you. Stop referring to the workplace as family. Your boss is not a surrogate parent. You alone are responsible for your performance, attitude, happiness, progress, and motivation.

3. The employee/employer contract can be terminated when one party breaches the contract. In other words, employees get to keep coming to work if they meet the terms of the contract. The employee chooses to come to work if the terms and work conditions continue to be suitable. If the employer fails to pay the employee, to treat the employee fairly, the employee might stop working and sue the pants off the employer.

As stated previously, the leader does bear a responsibility for fostering an environment conducive to productivity, creativity, calculated risk taking, reward, and recognition. But we all know that there are supervisors who won't live up to this standard and will fail to meet their contractual obligation.

Will you allow your success to be tied to the supervisor's inadequacy? Will you remain resentfully dependent on this leader and blame the incompetent leader for your lack of growth? An empowered person will say, "hell, no!" They will find a way to continue to achieve their goals despite their sorry boss.

Sadly, many disempowered employees choose the path of least resistance because their FBS gets in the way and tricks them into believing they don't have options. They make statements like, "My supervisor doesn't empower staff. My supervisor doesn't motivate me." Stop blaming your supervisor for your lack of empowerment. Everything is a choice and everyone has choice. Many people wait to be empowered by someone and delay or fail to take action toward a desired goal.

Don't seek empowerment before you act. Act and you will be empowered.

If you happen to be fortunate enough to work in an oppressive environment or an environment not worthy of your genius—consider this a gift. This gift was designed and packaged especially for you. You get to decide what you want to do with this gift. The decision rests solely with you. Do not deceive yourself into thinking you will, or can, change the environment or your boss or your coworker.

I have seen this attempted repeatedly where a person in a miserable work situation, with a jerk boss or organizational culture, thinks that their unhappiness will change the culture. The employee is miserable, stressed, and angry but not going to give up. They choose to fight a losing battle believing that the entire organizational culture that has existed for decades will change because they cry foul. Not gonna happen! It's time to exercise iChoice. You have to make an intelligent, inspired, intentional, individual choice.

Intelligent Choice

People exercise intelligent choice when they assess and apply all available knowledge and experience and then test that knowledge with the spirit (gut/intuition) before making a decision. They don't let ego rule the day. They understand that the internal spirit, when listened to, is the right choice.

Inspired Choice

People know when a choice is inspired because it springs deep from within and it's almost unexplainable. It is different from a mind decision or even a heart decision. A mind and heart decision is dependent on ego and feelings. An inspired decision is divine and compels them to act.

Intentional Choice

Intentional choice is deliberate, purposeful, and made by design. People exercising intentional choice are confident and determined, seeking a specific outcome, while recognizing that the choice they made has a price associated with it. They focus on the reward, despite the risk, and they make the choice that's right for them.

Individual Choice

Empowered, self-led, mature people exercise individual choice. They understand on a spiritual level that they are always in control, no matter the circumstance. They own their choices and accept total personal responsibility (TPR) for the outcome.

4. You have choices. This is a profound statement. No one employee or employer should be held hostage. Everyone is empowered to act and liberate themselves. Many people don't believe this.

Disempowered employees are entitled employees. They somehow feel that they are not strong enough, smart enough, or talented enough to make things happen. So, instead, they choose to believe that because they are powerless to make things happen, those they perceive to have power must make things happen for them. They make excuses for why they are not earning as much money as they want, living in the neighborhood they want, taking the vacations they want, and on and on. Excuses of any kind are problematic.

We learned earlier that excuses are useless. Disempowered people live in the nation of toleration. They tolerate the following.

- Status quo versus growth and change
- Silence versus speaking truth to power
- What's handed to them versus what's available to them

- Being average versus being extraordinary
- Being unhappy versus thriving
- Abuse versus self-love and care
- Low wages versus prosperity
- Disrespect versus self esteem
- Discomfort versus change
- Chaos versus clarity
- Blame versus total personal responsibility

I often ask the disempowered what causes them to endure this suffering. I'm curious why they make choices that perpetuate pain versus choices that will lead to freedom. The conversation occurs something like this.

You don't seem happy on your job. Are you?

No.

Why do you stay?

Because I'm not going to let them run me away from here.

Is your staying helping or hurting you?

Hurting me. I'm stressed. I don't sleep well.

Ok, so why do you stay?

I want to make them change.

Do you think they (boss, coworkers, culture) will change?

I hope so.

Ok, but do you think it will change? Are you seeing any signs of it?

Probably not. No.

So, what do you think is best for you?

I'm not sure.

You know you have choices, right?

Blank stare with anger or tears . . .

You can stay and change your perception of the situation. You can develop more effective coping skills. You can stand your ground and continue as you are, but you seem like you are in a lot of pain. You can see this situation as a gift and make a life-altering and liberating change for yourself. What do you think about that?

But why should I have to change/leave?

You don't, but it seems like you are in a lot of pain and you don't think things will get better. And unless you learn better coping skills, why would you stay?

Thinking (reluctantly) *Yeah, I guess you're right.*

Ok, so let's focus on what's going to make you happy now. Forget about what your stupid boss and coworkers think.

This process helps move one from ego/head decisions to spirit/gut decisions. Remember I said your spirit will never hurt you. We need to listen closely to what our spirit is telling us. Is your spirit telling you to make a different choice? To go in a different direction? To simply stay still? There is no wrong answer. There is only what is right for you.

I'm a Hustler, Baby

Empowered employees are hustlers. A hustler is a person who is aggressively hardworking, who knows how to get around problems, who will stop at nothing to achieve their dreams.

Opportunities increase as they are taken.
—Sun Tzu

Empowered employees (hustlers) become excellent leaders. Traditional leadership is dead! Employeeship is the new leadership.

Employeeship is a form of empowered leadership that is demonstrated consistently, regardless of title, position, salary, or hierarchy. You can't be a great leader without first being a great employee and demonstrating employeeship.

Great employees don't tolerate the status quo. It's not that they won't tolerate it, it's that they can't because they are so committed to excellence. Employeeshippers are not deterred by extra work, fear of failure, or difficulty. Employeeshippers follow these eight steps of employeeship.

Step One: Understand the Employee/Employer Contract

The terms are amazingly simple. As an employee, you trade your talents, skills, and abilities for money. As an employer, you seek out the best people to provide talents, skills, and abilities to further your organizational needs. The employer provides the necessary tools, equipment, along with a clean and safe workspace to perform the skills. When employees perform, the employer pays them. That's it, folks! Anything more is icing and the employee and employer should be mutually grateful.

This is not to negate the importance of cooperative relationships, respect, etc. All of these things make work more fun. My point is that it is not a mandatory part of the contract. If you want it, but are not getting it, then you have a choice to make. Members of the organization don't need to be your best friends. They are not and should not be considered family. They don't have to worry about your personal life. It's a business. If there is a problem with the terms, the contract might end.

A great employee understands this and comes to work every day working to fulfill the contract. Of course, the employer needs to do certain things to keep up its end of the bargain. But we're not talking about the employer here, are we? We are talking about *you*. Let's stay focused. Mind your business!

Step Two: Anticipate Needs

You don't have to tell employeeshippers what to do. You don't have to walk them through each step of a process. You don't have to keep asking them whether they considered this or that. Employeeshippers go beyond checking the box or completing a task. They are hustlers. They are always thinking of the next move. Taking it just a step further, providing that little extra, doing just a little bit more. They use critical thinking skills and make logical conclusions about the next step, and they act on their conclusions.

So many employees approach their contracts doing what they think the supervisor wants. This often eliminates their need to think. It's so annoying when employees give an answer they think the employer wants instead of providing a critically thought-through response. They are playing it safe, which is to their detriment. They cheat themselves, the supervisor, and the organization of their brilliance. And they are breaching the contract.

An employeeshipper doesn't fall into this trap. As an employer, when you find employeeshippers, focus your time and energy on ensuring they stay. They are priceless. One method of doing this is through "stay interviews," a retention tool to keep the best and brightest within an organization. I learned of this concept through Dick Finnegan, the best-selling author who wrote *The Stay Interview* and *The Power of Stay Interviews*.

Step Three: Seek, Embrace, and Apply Feedback

Employeeshippers are self-empowered to be their best selves. This means that they are constantly seeking to improve. They ask for feedback. They appreciate the positive feedback. Who doesn't? But what they are most interested in is the area of improvement. You see, they are confident in what they do well. They want to know what they can do better. They are not content with being good, because they know they were born to be great.

When they get feedback—whether it's negative-negative or constructive-negative—they heed it and apply it. I had a boss, exceedingly early in my career, give me feedback that first made me mad and then brought me to tears. Looking back on it now, it's silly that I cried, but I was young and thought I was all that. To get negative feedback of any kind was an assault to my ego. Fortunately, I had a mother who taught me to take what's good and leave what's bad.

This meant I needed to listen to the part of the feedback that had merit. Embrace it and self-correct. If the feedback was completely untrue, delivered for the purpose of crushing, instead of elevating, dismiss it. The key is reflection and alignment. If you have any self-awareness or emotional intelligence, you know when something is true. You might want to reject it, deny it, ignore it, or defend it, but that twinge in your gut (spirit) tells you otherwise.

Step Four: See Something, Say Something, and Do Something

Just like the agents tell you in the airport, if you see something, say something, for heaven's sake. Don't just sit there and wait till we all blow up. Employeeshippers not only see what needs to be done and draws attention to it, they initiate action to fix it. They have an intrinsic belief that if anyone can address the issue, it might as well be them. Juxtapose this belief with Suspicious Sally and Doubting Daniel, who intrinsically believe it's not their problem. They rest in their ignorant self-righteousness, knowing that they have the ability to improve a situation but simply refuse to do so—unless, of course, they are paid more money. They have yet to learn that money follows success, not the reverse.

Step Five: Take on the Difficult Stuff

No, employeeshippers are not masochists. They are not trying to unnecessarily abuse themselves, make their lives miserable, or inflict stress and pain. They thrive on challenge. They know that anything worth doing is often hard. It's not that they are working harder than anyone. Working harder is stupid. Working more effectively is brilliant.

They know that doing the difficult tasks builds muscles that others simply don't exercise. So, when the time comes for that promotion and big raise, they are well equipped to compete. They've been training while Suspicious Sally and Doubting Daniel have been moseying through their day saying, "That's not my job" and "I'll do it but they better pay me."

Step Six: Act as If

Employeeshippers act as if they are full owners of the company or a significant shareholder. They don't relegate a duty or function that they can handle to someone else. When you own a business, you do what needs to be done, no matter what, if it means increasing monetary and reputational profitability of your company. There is a certain pride that goes along with ownership. Employeeshippers know and love this pride. They say things like "This is my company." You'll see them do things like taking the initiative to workflow a process, seeking a more effective and efficient way of doing their work. They are invested. They are owners.

Step Seven: Recognize and Leverage Genius

Employeeshippers are self-aware. They know they weren't born to be good, but that they were born to be great. They've identified what they are fabulous at—not just what they are good at. The thing you do better and easier than most everyone else is your genius. I don't care what it is. It could be that your smile simply has a way of lifting everyone's mood. You can cut through FBS faster and more gracefully than anyone. You see clarity in utter chaos and you do it with ease. The things you play at, when someone else has to work extra hard at, are your genius. Employeeshippers don't try to be like someone else. They don't attempt to hijack someone else's genius or identity. They don't compete against others. They compete only against their best selves—continually getting better at being themselves.

Step Eight: Break the Rules

You can't be an employeeshipper if you don't break the rules. It's a requirement. If you are not breaking any rules, you are not working hard enough. You're playing it safe—too small. Employeeshippers are constantly challenging the status quo. They recognize that as time passes and expectations change, they have to keep reinventing themselves, improving processes, and introducing new concepts that are relevant for the current reality.

They don't rest on their laurels. They know that what got them here, won't get them there. They despise the concept of "If it ain't broke, don't fix it." They know that a five-pound mobile phone still allows you to make calls. But really? They know that a horse and buggy will still get you from point A to point B. But come on! They know that a town crier can still share news in the street. But, ok, that's ridiculous when we have a plethora of communication mediums. Employeeshippers aren't reckless freaks. They are, however, obsessed with excellence, and they take calculated risks to continue to push the envelope and raise the bar.

CHAPTER 8

Encore

I know I'm on overdrive on this subject, but I'm compelled to say a bit more about this overreliance on the boss. Listen up, all entitled brats. Engagement and empowerment cannot be done unto you. You decide to exercise employeeship and your power to think, create, meet, and exceed the terms of the contract.

If you don't like the terms of the contract, it is up to you to communicate your dissatisfaction, renegotiate the terms, or liberate yourself from the situation. It's all you, boo! Don't think your supervisor has to make your job or life better for you. This makes no sense, yet so many endorse this belief. It's a dangerous proposition.

I have learned that you cannot motivate anyone. As stated previously, motivation comes from within. You have to want to be better and do better. This desire must override any obstacles (such as a horrible supervisor) that might get in your way. If you want the promotion, the pay raise, the recognition, in other words a bigger contract, you have to work for it.

You can't just wait and hope that the boss will notice you or that your number will eventually be called. You are not a piece of meat in the deli. No one's going to just select you from the deli bin. The time you've spent in your seat will not cut it. Seniority policies kill productivity and reward time in position instead of contributions made while in the position.

Ever heard of the law of diminishing returns? Some of the least productive employees are those with the greatest seniority, yet many feel they are entitled to certain things simply based on their tenure. Sadly, we have empowered the sense of entitlement instead of fueling empowerment. Without constant reinvention of self, your contribution wanes, becomes outdated. Your supervisor shouldn't have to ask, like the Janet Jackson song, "What have you done for me lately?"

We've already established that I get frustrated with entitled brats. Giant babies are not cute. If you are over seven years old and needy, always trying to get attention by throwing tantrums, moping around with a sad frowny face, or displaying any typical childlike behavior, news flash: you are getting on everyone's nerves. Everyone knows that this behavior is a form of manipulation. You're avoiding the adult, difficult stuff. Reread step five of employeeship and get yourself together, please!

CHAPTER 9

It's Not Your Boss's Fault, Fool

You don't need to rely on your boss to validate you. It's not healthy to link your worth and value on how your boss, or anyone for that matter, treats you. Many confuse leadership with parentship. You will never get from your supervisor that which can only come from within—your self-worth.

Stop the blame game. Disempowered employees blame. They blame everyone but the person in their stupid selfie pic. So many of us fail to see the errors of our own ways but point out every little flaw in someone else. Every day I hear employees complaining and whining about management.

Who is management, anyway? It's like the elusive "they." Who is "they"? They is you, fool. Management is you, and you are failing miserably in managing your life. Comprende? Heard of self-management? When you manage yourself, others won't have to. When you elevate others who you perceive to be management, you diminish yourself. You are banishing yourself to a lower status.

You pretend to want to grow and promote, but truly you're more comfortable dabbling in dribble. Your mouth is constantly open and slowly allowing slimy disgusting dribbles of blame to flow from your lips. It's simply easier to blame your lack of success and happiness on the boss than to take total personal responsibility (TPR) for the outcomes in your life. My advice to you: wipe your mouth, please. Dribble is not a good look, and it's grossing me out.

You are 100 percent responsible for how you react to life events. If you drag yourself to a place you despise day after day, instead of choosing to change the situation, you have chosen to reside in Victimhood. You are not practicing iChoice—intelligent, inspired, intentional, individual choice.

Remember the employee/employer relationship is a contract. When the contract standards and terms are not met, it's time to move on or renegotiate the contract. Either way, the iChoice is yours.

CHAPTER 10

Obstruction Junction

Obstruction Junction is a place in Limbo Land. It's a horrible, wicked place. Trust me, you don't want to visit, and if you find yourself there, you don't want to stay. Unfortunately, many make the wrong choice and end up in this miserable land. Unlike the itsy bitsy spider, they never make it out again. They reside there until they die. It's spooky scary.

You know you're a Limboite when you're irrationally loyal to anything contrary to Limbo Land values. Limboites value the status quo, what's easy. They don't move forward or backward. They are in limbo. They robotically and instantly reject any idea that would free them from this hellish place or break the hypnotic spell. For certain, Suspicious Sally and Doubting Daniel live there. Despite the scary-looking people with permanent negative expressions and frowny, angry faces. Despite the fact that these people double as massive barricades impeding movement and progress, Sally and Daniel are quite comfortable.

There is comfort in misery. Remember, they believe they are great. They believe they are smart. They are skilled at finding all sorts of ways why an idea won't work and blocking progress at all cost. News flash: This is not a sign of being smart. This is a sign of being lazy. It will always be easier to find a reason not to do something versus finding a way to do something that is different, controversial, or challenging.

As humans, we are simply prone to inertia. Apparently, this stems from cave days when conserving energy was necessary for survival. Because we no longer live in the hunter-gatherer era, some folks have evolved from the energy-conserving mode and exert energy by taking action. Many, however, are still content in their inaction.

Do you want to know a secret? Smart people spend their time identifying how things can actually work. Failure, temporary setbacks, potholes, and road rage do not stop their momentum. They spur them on to try harder, to try differently. This is an important element of success. They don't keep doing the same thing over and over again and expecting different results. They keep tweaking, modifying, and evolving.

Imagine if Albert Einstein only focused on how relativity couldn't work. Imagine if Thomas Edison focused on how electric light couldn't work? Imagine if H.B. Reese, the genius who invented Reese's Peanut Butter Cups, focused on how peanut butter and chocolate couldn't be delicious . . . now that would be disastrous!

REFLECTION

Are you at Obstruction Junction? Describe the situation.

_____

_____

_____

_____

_____

_____

What iChoice will you make to get out of Limbo Land?

_____

_____

_____

_____

_____

_____

_____

PART 3:

....

Your Future Life— Don't Ask, Just Do!

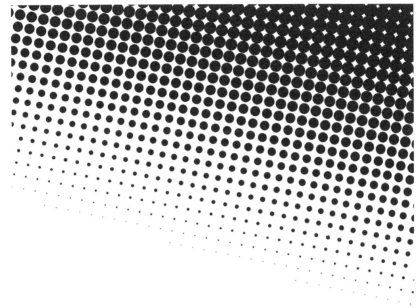

CHAPTER 11

Positive Rebellion?
Hell, Yes!

Stop asking permission to take every step. Many people feel they need approval from someone else to make a move. The problem with this is that because most people are risk averse, don't understand your vision and genius, and are living in their own fear, the response you get will be limited and framed within their limitations.

To get more done and to make more progress, sometimes you just need to do—not ask.

You've heard it said that it's better to ask for forgiveness than ask for permission.

When you ask for permission to be you, you will never be you.

It's crab mentality, a way of thinking described by the phrase "If I can't have it, you can't either." You will not be allowed to blossom, to flourish. People will pull you back so they won't be left behind. What's sad is that the alternate and better choice would be to tag along on the upward journey so everyone can rise. Don't get jealous, get clingy. Cling to everything people on the rise say and do and see how you can apply it.

A mentor once told me to only listen and take advice from those who have what you want. Don't listen to a broke person tell you how to get wealthy, or an unhealthy person tell you how to get in shape. Don't listen to a disempowered complainer tell you how to achieve your goals.

It's ok to be the single, beautiful daisy growing in the middle of a desert highway. It braves the heat, the violent traffic, and all odds working to eliminate its existence. Nothing or no one is able to extinguish it. It bends and folds with the passing of the speeding cars but stands strong in its purpose.

It's ok to be a giant in a land of miniatures, to be an eagle among the chickens. Don't get upset or derailed when the miniatures and the chickens fulfill their jobs brilliantly. Their job is to try to neutralize the situation, level the stakes, and reduce you to their size and purpose. They might peck at the fringes; they are designed to derail and to distract. You can just secretly smile when you experience small behavior. Commit to rise above it. Focus on your task to soar.

Stop doing what other people do as they are going with the flow.

Successful people and people who fill their life's purpose swim upstream.

Don't follow the herd, giving in to someone else's expectations, doing things that you don't want to do, when you know it's not good for you and doesn't align with your mission. If you don't like your results now, but you continue to do the same things that got you these results, you're insane or lazy.

Do the opposite of what you're doing now to get different results.

No excuses.

It's ok to rebel against anything that gets in the way of your purpose. Lisa Marie Selow, author of A *Rebel Chick Mystic's Guide*: *Healing Your Spirit with Positive Rebellion*, identifies ways to practice positive rebellion. I've listed a few of my favorites here.

1. Be happy now.

Don't delay your happiness until you have the right body, job, romantic partner, house, or car. If you base your happiness on external conditions, it's a sure way to disempower yourself. Material things wear out and conditions and people are changing. True, lasting, happiness comes from within. Happiness is a choice. Choosing happiness is the ultimate form of positive rebellion. You can choose to be happy, even if those around you are angry, depressed, negative, or whiny. Be so happy that even outer conditions such as a struggling economy or job market can't affect your happiness.

2. Let go of your childhood pain.

Don't hold onto old hurts. Liberate yourself by forgiving your parents and caretakers. Rebel against your own resentment, anger, sadness, or frustration. Forgiveness does not mean that you condone others' unloving behaviors. It's releasing the negative associations in your mind and heart, so that you can feel lighter and more peaceful. You don't even have to directly forgive the person. Just let go in your mind. It's a process, so you[r] forgiveness may not happen overnight.

3. Stop trying so hard to please everyone.

Set some boundaries with love. . . . Taking care of yourself is not selfish, but it may take some time for loved ones to adapt. Be rebellious and do it anyway, before stress affects your physical body. It's okay to say, "I'd love to help you, but not at this time."

4. Shift your "crap-itude."

Crap-itude is a term . . . to describe having a crappy attitude. Having a positive mental attitude and happiness are closely related. If you focus on what is wrong in your own life and in the world, happiness will elude you. Rebel against your inner crap. Some days, you may even have to fake it until you make it. Reject the negativity of the past in your mind, ditch your inner critics, and stop worrying about the future.

5. Be seen and be heard.

Sometimes women (and men) grew up with someone giving them the limiting belief that they should "be seen and not heard." At times, well-meaning authority figures try to quiet or even silence children. Yet, the world needs you to speak up and express yourself. There are causes of all sizes and varieties that need your help. If you don't express yourself, others miss out on your creativity, brilliance, and wisdom. Rebel against the tendency to silence your inner truth. (Of course, share it with love and respect.)

6. Live your purpose right now.

Instead of wondering what your life purpose is or having angst about not living it, take charge! Think of your top three favorite activities or hobbies. Look for clues about your life purpose. Sometimes, your life purpose varies from your job. You don't have to necessarily be paid doing something for it to count as your life purpose. Maybe you rock out on a drum kit on nights and week-ends, but your day job is cleaning houses? You might be a professional, such as a dentist, who teaches yoga on the side. You don't have to wait until your day job and life purpose are perfectly aligned. (Of course, don't quit your day job. Please, make sure you can pay your bills.) Again, be a positive rebel by not delaying your happiness until you create some outer condition in your life.

Are you ready for your selfolution, a revolution of self? It's a sudden, radical, or complete change and the reinforcement of self-leadership and empowerment. It's about to happen. Correction, it's happening already. As stated in the beginning, if you apply even a small portion of the information shared with you in this book, your life will change. Small behavioral changes compounded over time will get you to your destiny.

Write down five ways you will practice iChoice and when you will start.

_____

_____

_____

_____

_____

_____

Remember part of iChoice is intentional choice. You have to be intentional about your metamorphosis. Writing things down is one of many ways to increase accountability. It's up to you now. You've been armed with invaluable information. As poet Maya Angelou said, "When you know better, you do better." It's your choice.

Bonus Tips, Quips, and Other Radical and Random Rants

☆ Be excellent where you are. Don't think that once you get the job, promotion, or recognition, then you'll step it up. This is backward thinking and a form of entitlement. You give your power away when your actions are dependent on someone else's action. It is foolish and is equivalent to saying, "I'll be a good person when you think I'm a good person." Sounds stupid, doesn't it?

☆ If you hate your job, do yourself a favor and stop torturing yourself, your peers, and your employer—quit.

☆ "The human ability to rationalize, defend, and accept our self-imposed drama is bananas." —Jen Sincero

☆ Capitalize on nonmonetary currency (relationships, position, opportunity).

☆ Be aware of and examine your thoughts—ask why you are feeling a certain way. What is the underlying belief? You are responsible for your feelings. A person can't make you feel a certain way; you feel a certain way about a situation because of your belief and interpretation of the situation.

☆ "Smart people usually talk about things instead of people." —Larry Winget

☆ Conformity can be your worst enemy—just doing what the crowd does. If you continue to do this, you can predict with some certainty where you will be in twenty years. You will be exactly in the same spot, just twenty years older, unless you decide to increase your consciousness and take intentional steps toward identifying, visioning, and achieving your goals.

☆ If it's not HY (hell, yeah), it's bye.

☆ "A boss has the title; a leader has the people." —Simon Sinek

☆ "Make all conditions serve you." —David Gikandi

☆ The least conscious person of a group will bring down the experiences of the most conscious. So, it is in our best interest to help raise the consciousness of everyone.

☆ What I do unto others, I do unto myself.

☆ "All fears are generated by your ego not by your capability." —Darren Hardy

☆ The success of the organization is everyone's responsibility. I reject any notion that it is not.

☆ "Life will organize around the standards you set for yourself." —Darren Hardy

☆ We teach people how to treat us.

☆ A leader of self is a leader of many—lead by example.

☆ Gratitude is a characteristic.

☆ "If you want to be happy, you have to give up everything that makes you unhappy." —Larry Winget

☆ "Stress comes from knowing what is right and doing what is wrong." —Larry Winget

☆ When people ask me how long I plan to stay at a job, my answer is that I'm 100 percent committed until I'm not.

When I'm no longer having fun, when I feel I am not making the contribution I want to make, then I have to quit. This is the responsible thing to do for me, my team, and the company. Sadly, too many people are miserable at work (they are creating the misery, by the way, but, of course, they are blaming someone else for their experiences in life), and they continue to go to work most days and gripe, complain, and moan.

☆ Figure out how to add value to your boss's life, and your life will improve. I stopped believing that my job was just a job a long time ago. In fact, I'm not sure if I ever looked at it as just a job. But it wasn't until further in my career that I started to see my work as a mission. This really helped me get through the tough times where my coworkers were deliberately trying to make my life miserable. People who try to make your life miserable are themselves miserable. I learned to thank God for them because if it weren't for their attacks on me, my work, and my reputation, I might not have developed the toughness of spirit that I have today.

☆ Don't penny pinch. Don't be one of those employees who expects to be paid for doing something slightly above their job grade. I know people who expect to get paid for covering for a colleague for just a few hours! Not days, weeks, months, or years. Even days or a few weeks is greedy in my opinion. Of course, people should be paid fairly for the work they do, but can you imagine keeping score and charging for every little extra thing you do for someone? There is a horrible airline that does this. The prices for their flights are low, so you get tricked into thinking it's a good deal, until you want to carry your purse on the plane and they charge you. You want a cup of water and they charge you. This is ridiculous, and I will never fly with that airline again. When an employee asks for more money for doing a short-term assignment, you have to question their commitment to the work. They are too shortsighted to realize that the short-term assignment provides an opportunity to shine and to gain priceless experience that no one can ever take away.

☆ Don't be committed to misery. Some people are so committed to being miserable, they revel in it and seek it out at every turn. This misery gives them reward. Only until it becomes painful enough, or they become enlightened enough by reading a book like this, or by someone caring enough to tell them to wake up, will they start to redirect.

☆ "Intelligent individuals learn from every thing and every one; average people, from their experiences. The stupid already have all the answers." —Socrates

☆ Successful people don't follow money; money follows successful people.

☆ You will always take care of your priorities. I know what a person really believes in, cares about, has prioritized by what they do. Most people prioritize the trivial and then complain they don't have time to do the meaningful. The truth is you care more about TV, resting, taking the path of least resistance in your state of laziness than accomplishing the things you say you want—happiness, prosperity, and freedom.

☆ If you are not making mistakes and failing sometimes, you are not trying hard enough. You are playing it safe. No one ever accomplishes their dreams by playing it safe unless their dream is to stay miserable. If that's you, congratulations, you win.

☆ "If you could kick the person in the pants responsible for most of your trouble, you wouldn't sit for a month."—Theodore Roosevelt

☆ I live with no regrets. Even the mistakes I've made when I made decisions that a little small voice warned me about, I owned up to the mistake, showed gratitude for it, and moved on, never letting myself feel guilt or regret. Guilt and regret are a horrible drain on the brain. They make you feel hopeless and helpless. That is why I'm committed to being in a state of iChoice, constantly making intelligent, inspired, intentional, individual choices.

☆ "Do more of what you love, less of what you tolerate and none of what you hate." —John Assaraf.

☆ My purpose is to uplift and uplevel everyone to greater heights of achievement through honesty with compassion.

☆ "Entitlement = wanting. Never be in a state of want. Wanting creates conditions of perpetual wanting." —David Gikandi

☆ No one is better at being you than you.

☆ The real harm is the harm we do to ourselves when we are too afraid to be who we really are.

☆ Can you just get over yourself and get on with being your-self? Be who you are designed to be—full of purpose and prosperity and joy. You are getting in the way of you, and misery doesn't wear well. It is out of season.

☆ There are two parts to empowerment. I can give you the space, the permission, to be empowered, but you also have to be empowered to recognize, accept, and embrace the empower-ment. Many people are empowered to act, but because they are in a state of disempowerment, they choose not to act.

☆ I no longer entertain bitch-and-moan meetings. I eagerly welcome creative problem-solving meetings. What problem are we trying to solve?

☆ Every personal or organizational change/transformation effort must start with why. We have to always know first what problem we are trying to solve, so that we exert our energy, efforts, and resources in the right direction. When we establish our big, audacious goals, we need to understand the underlying *why*. If we are simply establishing a goal or aim because we think that's what we should be doing, then we will not be inspired and motivated to continue to swim upstream when things get tough. Things will get tough. Nothing worth working for is easy. So, if you think you should get that doctoral degree, go for that promotion, take on that assignment because you think that's what you are supposed to do versus digging deep within and discovering what you know you are supposed to do, then you alone have set yourself up for more unhappiness.

☆ Everything matters. Nothing ever goes to waste.

☆ "To the extent that you allow other people's choices and consciousness to override your own you will share in their consequences. I don't care does not exclude you." —David Gikandi.

☆ Everything you need is inside of you.

☆ "Stupidity is not the lack of knowledge but the illusion of having it." —Grigore Julian

☆ "It doesn't matter what comes after 'but'—all that matters is that it stops you from accomplishing something." —Katie Berbert

☆ Real growth happens when you choose to invest in yourself.

☆ Don't mistake activity for action or progress. Activity without focus is regression, not progression.

☆ Constantly compete against your own best self and measure your progress against your status of yesterday. Are you better today than you were yesterday?

☆ Light bulb: When people tell you the truth, sometimes it is annoying and painful.

☆ Cut out the FBS already. Your faulty belief system is holding you back.

☆ "Most people never realize their dreams because they didn't have the guts to risk the life that they are living for the one that they are capable of." —Darren Hardy

✫ You can always tell what a person truly believes by their results.

✫ Act and believe as if the world is conspiring to help you.

✫ Successful people don't follow money; money follows successful people.

✫ Don't seek empowerment before you act. Act and you will be empowered.

✫ "Opportunities increase as they are taken." —Sun Tzu

✫ To get more done and to make more progress, sometimes you just need to do—not ask. When you ask for permission to be you, you will never be you.

✫ Successful people and people who fill their life's purpose swim upstream.

✫ Do the opposite of what you're doing now to get different results.

ABOUT THE AUTHOR

Lori Gentles is a high energy, self-starter on a mission to help great people become greater. A radical believer in the power of intelligent, intentional, inspired, individual Choice (#iChoice), she parlayed her years of experience as a human resources leader to start The Choices Company. Her flagship program, Employeeship, The Path to Leadership, is a refreshing departure from the conventional and reinforces total personal responsibility instead of entitlement. Her message of iChoice and her commitment to helping highly self motivated individuals pursue possibilities without limitation has garnered the praise of peers and business leaders. "What you own, you can change" is her motto.

More on Lori Gentles

For more information about Lori, visit www.thechoicescompany.com. Connect with and follow Lori and the tribe of like-minded self-motivated achievers on instagram @weareichoice.

To have Lori Gentles speak to your organization about the principles found in *Oh Slap!* or other self-leadership insights, visit www.thechoicescompany.com.

Made in the USA
Las Vegas, NV
04 March 2021